FINANCIAL DELIVERANCE

DR. D.K. OLUKOYA

© 2012 A.D. – FINANCIAL DELIVERANCE
Dr. D.K. Olukoya

ISBN-13: 978-0615968988

A Publication of
TRACTS AND PUBLICATIONS GROUP
MOUNTAIN OF FIRE AND MIRACLES MINISTRIES
13, Olasimbo Street, off Olumo Road,
(By UNILAG Second Gate), Onike, Iwaya.
P.O.Box 2990, Sabo, Yaba, Lagos, Nigeria.
08023308127, 01-7747198, 01-7303485
Website: www.mountainoffire.org
E-mail: mfmhqworldwide@mountainoffire.org

I salute my wonderful wife, Pastor Shade, for her invaluable support in the ministry. I appreciate her unquantifiable support in the book ministry as the Cover designer, Art editor, and Art advisor.

All rights reserved. No part of this publication may be reproduced, stored in a retrieval system, or be transmitted in any form, or by any means, mechanical, electronic, photocopying or otherwise without the prior written consent of the publisher. It is protected under the copyright laws.

First Edition

FINANCIAL DELIVERANCE

Table of Contents

Chapter One
THE DIVINE PROSPERITY AGENDA..................................1

Chapter Two
THE SPIRIT OF MAMMON 9

Chapter Three
SIGNS OF THOSE WHO HAVE BEEN CAPTURED BY THE SPIRIT OF MAMMON..30

Chapter Four
REASONS WHY PEOPLE SUFFER FROM FINANCIAL BONDAGE..45

Chapter Five
HOW TO OBTAIN FINANCIAL FREEDOM..........................64

FINANCIAL DELIVERANCE

Chapter ONE

THE DIVINE PROSPERITY AGENDA

FINANCIAL DELIVERANCE

THE DIVINE PROSPERITY AGENDA — 2

Jesus came to break the backbone of poverty

FINANCIAL DELIVERANCE

THE DIVINE PROSPERITY AGENDA

It is a tragedy when the employer becomes an employee. It is a tragedy when the car owner is trekking. The Lord is the creator of heaven and earth. The Bible says, "The earth is the Lord's and the fullness thereof." If truly He is our Father and we are His children, He would not see His own children suffering and would say, "Well, continue."

In Luke 4:18, Jesus was reading from the book of Isaiah. He said, "The Spirit of the Lord is upon me because He has anointed me to:
1. To preach the gospel to the poor.
2. To heal the brokenhearted.
3. To preach deliverance to the captives
4. To preach recovery of sight to the blind.
5. To set at liberty those that are bruised.
6. To preach the acceptable year of the Lord.

Notice that when the Spirit of the Lord was

upon Him and He had been anointed, the first thing the anointing did had to do with poverty; to preach the gospel to the poor. Jesus came to break the backbone of poverty; to preach the gospel to the poor, and poor here means poverty in all its ramifications, for example, spiritual poverty, financial poverty, physical poverty, mental poverty, marital poverty etc.

He had been anointed to preach the gospel to the poor. It is on record that every country, whose foundation was built on the gospel, is prosperous. Any country where the gospel is given a free flow always experiences prosperity. Prosperity is attached to the gospel.

2 Corinthians 8:9 says, *"For ye know the grace of our Lord Jesus Christ, that, though he was rich, yet for your sakes he*

became poor, that ye through his poverty might be rich."

Finance has to do with money. Let us look at somebody in Matthew 27:3-5: *"Then Judas, which had betrayed him, when he saw that he was condemned, repented himself, and brought again the thirty pieces of silver to the chief priests and elders, saying, I have sinned in that I have betrayed the innocent blood. And they said, What is that to us? See thou to that. And he cast down the pieces of silver in the temple, and departed, and went and hanged himself."*

Money put this fellow in trouble. The money was useless to him and he threw it back at the temple. We need to strike a balance.

FINANCIAL DELIVERANCE

THE DIVINE PROSPERITY AGENDA

Money is paper and coins with value printed on them. It is the most acceptable form of exchange. Money is your sweat, energy, gift and blood.

WHAT IS FINANCIAL DELIVERANCE?

Financial deliverance means seven different things:
1. Freedom from debt.
2. Eating what you want and not what y o u see.
3. Not being dependent on your parents or others for livelihood or sustenance.
4. Adequate provision for yourself and your family.
5. Having the basic needs of life met such as food, clothing and shelter.
6. Having more income than expenditure.
7. Ability to lend and not to borrow.

It is indeed the will of God for His children to be financially free but the enemy in his craftiness has made man to have a lopsided view about money in order to gain control of him.

FINANCIAL DELIVERANCE

Prayer Points

1. Thou poverty distributor, I bury you today, in the name of Jesus.
2. Every strange money that has entered into my hands, backfire, in the name of Jesus.
3. Every power of mammon in my foundation, die, in the name of Jesus..
4. Satanic cobwebs harassing my destiny, roast, in the name of Jesus.
5. Put your hands in your pocket or handbag and pray like this: "Thou power of leaking pocket (or bag) die, in the name of Jesus.
6. Gold and silver come. Iron and brass, go, in the name of Jesus.
7. Yoke of poverty, break, in the name of Jesus.

FINANCIAL DELIVERANCE

Chapter TWO

THE
SPIRIT
OF
MAMMON

FINANCIAL DELIVERANCE

THE SPIRIT OF MAMMON — 10

It is wrong to pursue something that ends immediately you die. Money should not drive you out of this world before your time

THE SPIRIT OF MAMMON

Luke 16:13 says, *"No servant can serve two masters: for either he will hate the one and love the other, or else he will hold to the one, and despise the other. Ye cannot serve God and mammon."*

You cannot serve God and mammon.

Money has put human beings into a battle that has no end. Money has been the subject of pursuit since man came into the world. Money has turned itself into the greatest idol. Majority of people have been captured in the school of money worship. Many have gone to where they should not have gone. Many have swallowed what they should not have swallowed because of money. Many have befriended who they should not have befriended because of money. Many are suffering in strange lands now because of money.

Money is a deceiver, it causes sicknesses that cannot be healed. Money causes a lot of confusion. Those who do not have it think they are in trouble, and of a truth, they are really in trouble. Those who have it are in trouble too. It has deceived many girls into breaking their virginity in shame.

Money is very terrible. It has made many to suck blood in occult camps. It has changed the calling of God on very many people. It has sent many souls to untimely grave. If we remove money in circulation, the rate of high blood pressure will go down. Money has turned so many young women to widows and many children into orphans. It has a caging influence.

There is a spirit known as mammon. It is the spirit behind inordinate love for money. A certain man travelled to India in search of the power to make money magic. He had resolved that at whatever cost, he must be rich. If others were making it, he must make it too. If it would be blood money, he would not care. He wanted it at all cost. Somebody introduced him to the place. When he came home, he built an altar in his bedroom, where he worshipped the power behind the occult wealth. At midnight, a serpent would crawl out of that altar and vomit money, millions of naira. But the covenant he had with the serpent was that any day it asked for something, he must give it, and they agreed.

The man bought five V-Boot Mercedes Benz cars in one day, and many people were wondering where he got his money. But the word of God that says, "Do not envy the rich," is a very powerful word. One day, after the serpent had vomited money, instead of it to disappear into the altar as usual, it spoke and said, "I want something." The man said, "What?" It said, "Go and bring your boy that is at the Federal Government College, that is what I want." That was the boy the man loved most and the brightest of his children. He said, "Serpent, take the mother" (that is his wife). The snake said, "No, I do not want the mother." The man said, "I cannot bring the boy here." Immediately he refused, the serpent went back into the altar in anger, the altar broke into two and the man fell down and could not walk again. They began to carry him from place to place until one day, he died.

The second person who collected the same power from India, when he saw the cheap way his colleague died, ran to Mountain of Fire and Miracles Ministries. He said to me, "Man of God, help me to clear the altar in my bedroom." I said, "Am I the one who put it there for you?" He eventually went through deliverance and those things were burnt and God delivered him. Today, when he hears anything about money, he would close his ears and walk away.

Beloved, your life is more than money. You met money in this world and you will leave it and go. It is wrong to pursue something that ends immediately you die. Money should not drive you out of this world before your time. Anytime they say, "Money," some people begin to develop high blood pressure, their body temperature rises and their brains begin to calculate what they ought to have. But the Bible says that money is made for you, and not you for money.

Money has destroyed the calling of many men of God. Money has destroyed what so many people stand for. It has destroyed the destiny of so many people. No wonder the Scripture says that you cannot serve God and mammon. The reason many people do not attend some church meetings is that they are looking for money. Some people cannot attend vigils because they are doing overtime. They are looking for money. Unfortunately, they do not know that a single boil in the leg can take away every kobo that they have in their bank accounts.

I know somebody, a boil he had took N200,000 from his bank account. The day his pastor told him to bring one third of whatever he had in his bank account, he did not bring one kobo.

Everybody else did but he did not. He decided that his money must be intact. It is foolishness to put money in fixed deposit when the work of God is suffering. Anyone who has that attitude can be killed by the same money. Money can kill.

Why should somebody kill his own wife because of money? I have seen many examples. I have also seen people who have killed their own mothers because of money. Quick money is quick death. Why don't you just work hard, be patient and wait upon God for your own time. The blessing of God makes rich and adds no sorrow to it. It is better to have a little with peace than having the whole world but you are in trouble.

THE WEALTH OF SORROW

There is wealth, which the Bible calls the

wealth of sorrow. If you gather this type of wealth, you get into trouble. You cannot make the sun to rise before its time. Do not do any wrong thing to get money. If you do, you will vomit it. Even generations after you will vomit it. There is no peace in ill-gotten money.

Money has a voice, it speaks. To listen to that voice is to pick a cobra. It is an ancient power, which is very strong and very deceptive. It controls the foolish and makes them do all kinds of evils. It has deceived kings and confused nations. It has separated couples and removed trust from many marriages and homes. It has sent many souls to hell fire. It has made many girls and women mad. It has made them sell their bodies to men and animals. The truth is this, money that does not originate from God is a curse.

THE SPIRIT OF MAMMON

There is a spiritual force behind money. Believers may not understand it very well but unbelievers do. The Bible says, "Seek ye first the kingdom of God and his righteousness and all other things will be added unto you" (Matthew 6:33). That Scripture is telling us what our priority should be.

Most of those who run about trampling on this and that to make money do not really make it. Most of those who say they are smart will discover that the devil will outsmart them. Money is a deceiver. It has caused so much havoc. We been have warned that as long as we use our lives serving mammon, we cannot serve the true God.

THE HEAVY LOAD ON MONEY

Money carries a lot of heavy load. Take a dirty Naira note and look at it very well. It represents blood and sweat because it can serve man and can also destroy him. Many people cannot kiss a person who has HIV, but if he puts down a lot of money and says, "If you kiss me, you will get money," many people would quickly go and kiss him. They would not mind.

Only God knows how many hands have touched the money you are holding. You do not know the good and the evil the note in your hands has done since it was printed. You may be looking at the note as a piece of paper, but it may be hiding something from you. That money you are spending has sweat and blood on it and many people might have died because of it. It might have been the cause of somebody's HIV. Many people might have killed themselves for it. Only God knows how much havoc it has done moving from hand to hand. It might have bought somebody a wedding ring. It might have paid for a baptismal card. It might have paid for dresses for a growing baby. It might have paid for books for someone's education. It might have been the money used in buying stamps to send a letter to break somebody's heart. It might have paid for a film with the warning: "Not for children." It might have been used to record decent songs. It might have brought a few minutes or hours of enjoyment. It might have been used in paying for a weapon of crime. This is why you must always pray on your money before spending it. You never could tell where it came from. You may not know how much havoc it has caused.

THE ACTIVITIES OF MAMMON

It is the secret of mammon to trap people. It is the secret of mammon to get people caged and they are not able to get out. Mammon is the devil's sales man. It is responsible for the distribution of the spirit of poverty, especially to Christians. It controls the spirit of financial bankruptcy.

If you can defeat the spirit of mammon in your life, the power of breakthrough will flow into your soul. Many people need to bind this spirit. It is the spirit that grips many and makes them to become slaves. It causes people to develop bad habits and attitudes which they cannot get rid of. The Bible says that you cannot be neutral. You either serve God or mammon, you cannot serve two of them at the same time.

Therefore, one way to serve God is to re-examine your attitude towards money. Once your attitude towards money is wrong, you are on your way to hell fire. The Bible makes us to understand that where your treasure is, there your heart lies.

Many people have gathered millions of naira before we were born. Where are they now? I remember the story of that man who understood what spiritual prosperity means. He knew that if he could get spiritual prosperity, financial prosperity would just be a joke. Does the Psalmist not say, "Since I was young and now I am old, I have never seen the righteous being forsaken or his children begging bread." In many nations of the world where Christianity is deeply rooted, you do not see the children of God begging bread.

In the olden days, whenever banks wanted to employ people, they came to pastors to ask for people because they were sure that those men and women would not be bought over by mammon. That was many years ago. Today, a so-called born again man would be the first to start stealing. What does he want to do with the money? He would be the first to cooperate with thieves. Our God cannot do anything with that kind of money. You cannot eat more than one plate of food at a time. You cannot wear more than one suit at a time. If you put on four garments at a time, people will say that you are sick. You cannot sleep in four rooms at the same time.

The Lord has a purpose for providing for His children. If He looks at you and finds that mammon has captured your life, He will not prosper you because He knows that if He gives you financial breakthrough, you will not use it to promote His work. You may use it to commit more sin.

If you want more blessing from God, you must pray that the power of mammon operating in your life should die, in Jesus' name.

Romans 12:1-2 says, *"I beseech you therefore brethren, by the mercies of God, that ye present your bodies a living sacrifice, holy, acceptable unto God, which is your reasonable service. And be not conformed to this world but be ye transformed by the renewing of your mind, that ye may prove what is that good, and acceptable, and perfect will of God."*

If you do not present your body to the Lord, you will present it to something else. Certainly, something will use you. The Lord may use you, the devil may use you, or you may decide to use yourself. The reason many cannot sacrifice themselves to the work of the Lord is that they themselves are not sacrificed. But if you are already dead to self, you will give God anything. Then the things of God will be moving and God will be bombarding you with blessings.

Believers are poor because they are stingy when it comes to the things of the Lord. Judas got money, but the money was useless. He discovered that too late. The Bible calls mammon a god. You cannot serve it and God; it is impossible. You cannot work for two masters. You cannot carry a tree on both shoulders.

One day, somebody, who was very close to me before he went to be with the Lord prayed like this: "O God, I am tired of poverty. I want to be blessed." He prayed and fasted for three days. Then the Lord showed him a Bible and asked him to open it. He did and found brand new ten pounds notes. And the Lord said to him: "Your prosperity has to do with this book. If you drop it, you will die in poverty but if you work with it, you will prosper." This revelation would have been enough for this brother but no, he went and bought a bus on hire purchase. The bus started immediately to develop problems. One day, the police would arrest the driver. another day, the driver would be sick and would be unable to work. The day the driver was not sick, the conductor would steal all the money. At the end of the day, he got very little out of that bus but it brought problems, worry and tension. That is why when people come to me and ask for prayers for such a business, I always tell them to get ready for hard work, which includes anointing the vehicle when it returns at night and praying because of the kind of creatures it carries during the day. Any day they forget to do that, trouble would start. This is why a few people prosper in transport business.

When you are trying to know mammon instead of Master Jesus, you will discover that you have been captured. Your attitude towards money as a Christian is very important and should be examined thoroughly.

FINANCIAL DELIVERANCE

Prayer Points

1. Every dream of poverty, die, in the name of Jesus.
2. Angel of prosperity, locate my address, in the name of Jesus
3. O Lord, by the thunder of your power bring honey out of the rock for me, in the name of Jesus.
4. Ever altar of poverty in my family, I am not your candidate, therefore, die, in the name of Jesus.
5. Lintel of poverty, roast, in the name of Jesus.
6. It has been well said that people are poor due to poverty of ideas. So, put your right hand on your head and pray: Good and useful ideas, fall upon me, in the name of Jesus.
7. My brain, reject poverty, in the name of Jesus.

Chapter THREE

SIGNS OF THOSE WHO HAVE BEEN CAPTURED BY THE SPIRIT OF MAMMON

FINANCIAL DELIVERANCE

SIGNS OF THOSE WHO HAVE BEEN CAPTURED BY THE SPIRIT OF MAMMON

The good thing about banking in heaven is that you get even more money here and still get a mansion above

FINANCIAL DELIVERANCE

SIGNS OF THOSE WHO HAVE BEEN CAPTURED BY THE SPIRIT OF MAMMON — 32

If you have been captured by the spirit of mammon, you will have inordinate desire for money. You would pick money on the road. You would tell all kinds of lies to obtain it. Your ear would be deaf to the things of God and money will be the root of all evil in your life.

They told us the following story when we were much younger. Three thieves went to steal a bag of money. Having stolen the money, they were still not satisfied. Each of them wanted the money for himself alone. So, two of them planned against one. They sent him to buy food and decided to kill him when he came back. The one who went to buy the food also calculated how he could take the whole money. He decided to poison the food so that when the other two ate it, they would die. When he returned, they shot him dead and quickly ate the food before they would run away. Of course, two of them also died.

Money is capable of good and evil. The bottom line is this: you either rule money or it rules you. Whether you are poor or rich, you either rule money or it rules you. Poverty does not free one from the rulership of money. The attitude of some people who are living in poverty is worse than that of those who are rich. This is why a man may decide to put his money in his pocket and tell his wife that there is no money to buy essential things for the family.

The love of money can drive both the rich and the poor to stealing. It can turn them to thieves. The love of money makes some drivers to be involved in accidents. The absence of money would have made some people to live longer. Many of the afflictions some people are facing would not have been there if they have not loved money. There is a type of money that comes and removes money from you. As a believer, if the love of money is found in you, you need deliverance, because it will be difficult for God's blessing to fall upon you.

I know a man of God, who inherited a house from his mother. He was doing well before then but immediately he inherited this house, his finances went down and he became poor. The Lord said, "Do you know how your mother acquired the property? All the wealth was blood money and you added it to your own. That is the cause of your trouble." Until he abandoned the property, he did not prosper.
A lot of times pastors settle quarrels between brethren who are business partners. They

would have agreed before starting the business on how to share their profit. But when the profit is big, one would want to take everything or the lion's share. All the time, when we were young Christians, I did not see fellow Christians dragging themselves to police stations or the law courts. But nowadays I see many of them. This is the work of the demon of mammon, but the Bible says you cannot serve God and mammon together.

Men of God are not supposed to be begging but nowadays there are many pastors doing commercial vigils because of money. There are pastors advertising for vigils. They would says, "Madam, you need deliverance and vigil."

If you lose money and it is to you like losing a

FINANCIAL DELIVERANCE

SIGNS OF THOSE WHO HAVE BEEN CAPTURED BY THE SPIRIT OF MAMMON

human being, mammon has already captured your soul. If the absence of money is bad enough to lead you to say that you want to take your own life, mammon has already captured you.

A lot of people overestimate the power of money. But even the rich have discovered that there are certain things that money cannot buy. Some poor people imagine that once they have money, their problems are over. That is why we say that money can buy a bed but cannot buy sleep. It can buy you books but cannot buy you a brain. It can buy you medicine but cannot buy you health. It can build a church but cannot get you to heaven.

When money makes a person to bow to unscriptural circumstances, then mammon has captured his soul. The Bible says that you cannot serve God and mammon together. True riches are from God and are really spiritual. Some people spend 99 per cent of their energy running after money and the trouble is that they never really find it. Many believers are poor because they are very stingy with the Lord. So, the question is, have you turned God to a dustbin? That is you give God only what you do not need or what you cannot feel when you give. Have you made God a beggar?

Matthew 6:19-21 says, *"Lay not up for yourselves treasures upon earth, where moth and rust doth corrupt, and where thieves break through and steal. But lay up for yourselves treasures in heaven, where neither moth nor rust doth corrupt, and where thieves do not break through nor steal. For where your treasure is there will your heart be."*

This is a serious matter for a believer. If you stingily keep your money, you will lose it. Many years ago, I kept my money in a bank account somewhere. One day, to my amazement I went there and wanted to withdraw N3,000.00 and they said, "We can give you only N1,000." I said, "But I have N8,000 with you. They said, "N1,000 is all that we can give to you. You either take it or leave it." I said, "But it is my money." At this point, somebody tapped me at the back and said, "You better take it or you will not get anything." It was my money. I kept it there but they said I could not have it.

The world is bankrupt. You have to bank in heaven. The good thing about banking in heaven is that you get even more money here and still get a mansion above. God will not force you to part with your money.

When the spirit of mammon grips your heart and is poisoning you, you need deliverance. Do you inwardly cry because of money? Are you dissatisfied with yourself because of money? Do you go about worrying on how to make more money? If your answer is yes, you better go for deliverance.

The Bible says, "Seek ye first His kingdom and His righteousness and all other things shall be added unto you." If you do not seek first the kingdom of God and you are running after other things, sin is the result. If you refuse to keep your money in the heavenly bank, the enemy will help you to destroy what you have here on earth.

Mammon is a demon power in control of money. It is responsible for distributing the spirits of poverty to attack the human race, especially Christians. If you bow to the altar of mammon, he will give you money and with it, you sell your soul. But if you are a believer and do not want to bow to it, if it comes to attack you with the spirit of poverty, you can overcome it.

WHAT ARE THE SIGNS THAT THE SPIRIT OF MAMMON IS WORKING AGAINST YOU?

When you see snails, flies, bedbugs or rags in the dream, it is a sign that this spirit is working against you. When you see yourself naked or eating strange things, or you see cobweb, oil or pepper, or you see yourself distributing things to people, then know that the spirit of mammon is working against you.

If you lived in the village a long time ago and never ate cocoyam but now it is being offered to you in the dream, you need to pray. Or you see that anywhere you go, there is blockage, you cannot have financial breakthrough, you need to pray. The spirit of mammon is the power stealing your certificate in your dreams. You have to let the Lord move upon your life to dismantle this power.

If you notice that in your family there is no graduate, you should stand up and say, "My own case must be different." In some families anyone who builds a house must die. So, members of such families would be running away. There are thousands of people, whose children can only prosper if they do not stay in their villages. If they dare come home, they should be prepared for burial.

This world is already judged and I want you to understand it very well. If you focus on making money and not on making heaven, you become materialistic. If you do not care about how money is made, you just want it; it is still the grip of mammon.

The truth however is that all the quick money go away very quickly, and life on the fast lane usually ends very fast. Stealing, illegal work, cheating, defrauding, misappropriation, occult practices, demonic sacrifices, armed or pen robbery, and all the ungodly ways of getting money are signs of the grip of the spirit of mammon.

The Bible tells us that the power to get wealth comes from God and He wants us to be financially free. Jesus did not only die to save us from sin, He also came to save us from poverty. God can make you wealthy either by giving you money or by supplying your needs. He supplied the needs of Adam and did not give him money.

If God has apportioned wealth to you and you go and add a bit of unrighteousness to the way you seek your wealth, the result is that you will miss that divine wealth. And if you are not careful, you will not touch that wealth till you die. There are many people who come for counselling and immediately you see them, you will know that they were born with the anointing to be wealthy but it has been taken away.

There are some people whom others naturally look up to for financial assistance, they appear rich and wealthy but alas, they are poor and looking for help themselves. If you fall into this category, you need to pray.

FINANCIAL DELIVERANCE
Prayer Points

1. My pocket, reject leakage, in the name of Jesus.
2. Every dream of poverty, die, in the name of Jesus.
3. Anointing of poverty, die, in the name of Jesus.
4. Every witchcraft dog barking against my prosperity, what are you waiting for? Die, in the name of Jesus.
5. Power of wastage, die, in the name of Jesus.
6. Every spiritual rag working against my destiny, roast, in the name of Jesus.
7. My star, look not at your background. Arise and shine, in the name of Jesus.

Chapter FOUR

REASONS WHY PEOPLE SUFFER FROM FINANCIAL BONDAGE

FINANCIAL DELIVERANCE

REASONS WHY PEOPLE SUFFER FROM FINANCIAL BONDAGE — 46

The origin or foundation of the capital for your business has to be clean

WHY DO PEOPLE SUFFER FROM FINANCIAL BONDAGE?

1. Generational curse: Genesis 9:25: *"And he said, cursed be Canaan, a servant of servants shall he be unto his brethren."*

That is, a curse subjected Canaan to poverty. If your forefathers suffered from financial poverty, you need to pray aggressively because it means that there is a curse you need to break. You need to declare that others might be falling into it but your case must be different. It is a wrong foundation. The Bible says, "If the foundation be destroyed, what can the righteous do?" Also, you have to be careful of all the curses that come in the form of jokes. Somebody would look at his colleague and say, "It will not be well with you." This is a curse. It is not something you just accept. You must reject it. For example, it does not matter whether a descendant of

Canaan has accumulated millions of naira, he is under the curse of servant of servants, and has to break it in order to move forward.

2. Wrong foundation: Wrong business foundation, wrong academic foundation wrong certificate, wrong marital foundation etc will result in problems.

3. Too much responsibilities: When you are looking after so many things at the same time, you will have problems.

4. Unwise investment: When you invest into something that God did not ask you to do, there will be problems.

5. Living beyond your means.

6. Stealing and sharp practices.

7. Wrong job, wrong business: Many people are in the wrong jobs and wrong businesses and they are praying that God should bless the wrong jobs or wrong businesses that He did not ask them to do.

8. Lack of saving: Some people do not save anything. They spend everything they earn.

9. When you have more expenditure than income.

10. Stealing from God by not giving your tithe and offering: All successful men in the Bible were those who paid their tithes. When you do not pay your tithe, devourers will be released against you and they will swallow what you have. Tithe is one-tenth of whatever income you have. Some wise people give God more than that.

REASONS WHY PEOPLE SUFFER FROM FINANCIAL BONDAGE

12. Failure to honour pledges.

13. Disobedience to God's leading.

14. Living in debt: The debtor is always a slave.

15. Negative confession.

16. Demonic activities.

17. Laziness or what the Bible calls slothfulness: Proverbs 6:6-11 says, *"Go to the ant thou sluggard, consider her ways and be wise, which having no guide, overseer or ruler, provideth her meat in the summer, and gathereth her food in the harvest. How long will thou sleep, O sluggard? When will thou arise out of thy sleep? Yet a little sleep, a little slumber,* *a little folding of the hands to sleep, so shall thy poverty come as one that travelleth, and thy want as an armed man."*

Laziness will lead to poverty. Two brothers were retired in their places of work. One was a Christian and the other, an unbeliever. The Christian would sit in the house and pray or go out to witness, come back and sleep for the rest of the day. The unbeliever used the money he was paid to buy a table tennis board nearby and very soon people began to come and play tennis and to pay him some money for the facility. The Christian brother was not doing anything to earn money, so he was poor.

18. Satanic covenant to be poor physically but rich spiritually: There are some people, who have formed a covenant with some powers that they would have money and ride cars in the spirit realm but would be poor physically.

19. Inherited poverty: This is when a person comes from a family where poverty is the order of the day, the whole family is wallowing in poverty and it is being transferred from person to person.

20. Unprofitable assistance: If you are assisting the enemy of God, you will be rendered poor. There are some people who really must not be helped. You have to pray very well before giving out your money. You may end up in a serious problem if you assist an enemy of God. For example, you give somebody money for school fees and she uses it for abortion.

21. Altars of poverty: When an altar of poverty has been erected against a person and a decision taken that the person will never make it. You need to pull down that kind of altar. Do not be surprised that some people would go to a bank to borrow money and the bank would agree to lend them the money on the condition that they pawn their land and house documents. They would pawn these things and the bank would take them to the altar of poverty and say, "Thou altar of poverty, make sure that this one does not have money to pay us back so that we can take over his property." Eventually, he may not have the money to pay back and would forfeit his land and house.

22. Direct attack from satan: Job 1:13-19 says, *"And there was a day when his sons and his daughters were eating and* *drinking wine in their eldest brother's house. And there came a messenger unto Job and said, The oxen were plowing, and the asses feeding beside them; and the Sabeans fell upon them and took them away; yea, they have slain the servants with the edge of the sword; and I only am escaped alone to tell thee. While he was yet speaking there came also another and said, The fire of God is fallen from heaven, and hath burned up the sheep, and the servants, and consumed them; and I only am escaped, alone to tell thee. While he was yet speaking there came also another, and said, The Chaldeans made out three bands, and fell upon the camels and have carried them away, yea, and slain the servants with the edge of the sword; and I only am escaped alone to tell thee. While he was yet speaking, there came also another, and said, Thy sons and thy daughters were eating and drinking wine in their eldest brother's house. And, behold, there came a great wind from the wilderness, and smote the four corners of the house, and it fell upon the young men, and they are dead; and I only am escaped alone to tell thee."*

Satan systematically destroyed Job's property.

23. Habitual sin: When a person continually commits a particular sin. On Monday, he does it and cries to the Lord, "O Lord, forgive me." On Tuesday, he is back to it again. The person is writing a letter to poverty. Deuteronomy 28:15-16 says, *"But it shall come to pass, if thou wilt not hearken unto the voice of the Lord thy God, to observe to do all his* *commandments and his statutes which I command thee this day, that all these curses shall come upon thee, and overtake thee. Cursed shalt thou be in the city and cursed shalt thou be in the field."*

24. Pestilence and famine: These can cause poverty. The Psalmist who says that we should stand against pestilence and famine knows what he is saying.

26. Stinginess and selfishness: Proverbs 11:24 says, *"There is that scattereth, and yet increaseth; and there is that withholdeth more than is meet, but it tendeth to poverty. The liberal soul shall be made fat: and he that watereth shall be watered also himself."*

Sometime ago, I read the story of a man, who borrowed some money from his friend. For years, he refused to pay back, although the friend often asked for the money. One day, while they were relaxing in the friend's sitting room, an armed robber rushed in and said, "Bring all your money." Immediately, he put his hand in his pocket, brought out some money and said in the presence of the armed robber, "This is the money I am owning you, take it now." That is stinginess and selfishness. Some people are so stingy, even against themselves, and the enemy would come upon them with poverty.

I know a man, who deprived himself of good food and by the time he died, three thousand British pounds was found under his bed. If God sees that you have money and refuse to spend it, He will put you aside and bring another person who will spend it.

27. Lack of mercy: James 2:13 says, *"For he*

shall have judgment without mercy, that hath shewed no mercy; and mercy rejoiceth against judgment."

28. Territorial demotion in business: There are some territories or areas where certain businesses cannot prosper. A certain brother started a big business in a place but lost everything he brought into that business before he joined us in prayer. During prayers, the Lord said that the location of the business was the problem, that two pregnant women had been buried under the building and that there was no way anybody could prosper there. Meanwhile he had wasted thirteen years in that place. He went to the estate agent who found the place for him and asked him what he knew about the place and he answered, "Can't you see that the rent is low. When you took the shop I thought you would succeed there. People who rented other shops there have left. You are the only one remaining." The man asked, "Is it true that two pregnant women were buried there?" The estate agent said, "It could be more than that." The brother had to relocate his business before he began to prosper.

29. Demonic possession: When a demon is inside a person, as the person moves about, he distributes the spirit all over. If you employ a demonized person in your business, you will have problems. If you allow such a person to plait your hair, you too will be affected. So, you have to be very careful.

30. Keeping the company of a cursed person: if you are in a business partnership with a cursed person, you are courting trouble. When you are paying your own tithe to the Lord, he is paying his own to the devil, so, there will be problems.

31 Receiving strange money: Polluted money that comes into somebody's hand can take away the one that he already has.

32. Blood covenant: If you enter into a blood covenant for wealth, you are writing a letter to the spirit of poverty.

33. Demonic gift used as capital for business: If you take money from a sugar daddy to start a business, you will be poor. When you sell your body in order to get money to start a business, you are already finished. The origin or foundation of the capital for your business has to be clean. That is why when some people become born again, they first become poor, because God wants to evacuate the evil foundation of the money they have.

34. Unfaithfulness to a business partner: If you are cheating a business partner, you are writing a letter to poverty.

35. Mismanagement of fund: This leads to poverty.

36. Extravagance: When you behave as if you owned the whole world; you are extravagant in your dressing and in the way you spend money, you are inviting poverty.

37. Spirit of death: When this spirit enters, no matter what money the person is making, it is the hospitals that will collect it. Sometime ago, in America, a woman came to me, sat down and said, "I can't talk sir. Please read this paper." When I read the paper, I was quite surprised. I had never seen that kind of thing before. The doctor wrote that there were 26 sicknesses in her body. There was something wrong with her heart, lung, kidney, etc. I said, "But were you born like this?" She said, "Everything started one year ago." She had spent everything she had and was now poor.

38. Living in a demonic house: This is why it is good to pray that God should bless you so that you too can have your own house. It is not bad to live in another person's house, but when you do and the person living on top of your apartment is a witch, the one living by your side is bringing in one prostitute every night and the one living at the front is lighting demonic candles every night, you may be in trouble.

FINANCIAL DELIVERANCE

Prayer Points

1. Power of the most high God, kill my Pharoah, in the name of Jesus.
2. Anointing to prosper, fall upon my life, in the name of Jesus.
3. Every closed door in my life, hear the word of the Lord, open, in the name of Jesus.
4. I shall prosper whether the enemy likes it or not, in the name of Jesus.
5. Idol of poverty in my place of birth, die, in the name of Jesus.
6. Every owner of the load of poverty, die, in the name of Jesus.
7. The sun shall not smite me by day nor the moon by night, in the name of Jesus.

FINANCIAL DELIVERANCE

Chapter FIVE

HOW TO OBTAIN FINANCIAL FREEDOM

If God finds that He cannot withdraw from you, He will stop depositing in you

WHY DO WE NEED FINANCIAL DELIVERANCE?

1. To have a fulfilled life.
2. To manifest the glory of God.
3. To appropriate our redemption right.
4. The destiny of many people is attached to us and we need to carry their financial burden.
5. To be able to further the things of the kingdom of God.
6. Poverty is demonic and is a killer. Millions of people die of malaria every year but if poverty is removed, malaria will stop killing people. A lot of people cannot afford to buy insecticides for their homes and environments. What many do is to gather dry orange peels and begin to burn them as insecticides. They forget that mosquitoes which they are trying to eradicate like to eat oranges. The smoke

from the orange peels gets into their nostrils and they inhale it, thereby causing more problems all because of poverty.
7. To lay up treasures for ourselves in heaven.

It is your redemptive right to possess your possession. And it is time for you to realize that God in His arithmetic does not mind withdrawing things from unbelievers and giving them to His children.

HOW TO OBTAIN FINANCIAL FREEDOM
There are two ways to obtaining financial freedom:
1. Through your work.
2. Through giving to God.

The Bible says that he who does not work

must not eat. Man must work and work hard. God did not place man on earth to be lazy, indolent and jobless. Therefore, the number one condition for financial freedom is work. Whatever work you do must be God's idea. It must have a future.

Through giving to God: Many people have come to financial ruin simply because they do not give or do not give enough. Many people give grudgingly and they do it with strings attached. If God finds that He cannot withdraw from you, He will stop depositing in you. God expects you to pay your tithe and offering, sow seeds, pay your first fruits, sow into the ministry, promote the gospel, and take action with what He has given to you. If we say that we belong to God, it is logical that everything we have belongs to Him. When we give to God, what we are doing is taking our hands off what belongs to Him. If you cheat God and say you are economizing, you are economizing to poverty.

Your attitude towards money shows what you think of God. Those who refuse to pay their tithes do not have the problem of money but that of spiritual blindness. He, who serves God because of money, will serve the devil for bigger wages. When God gives you a talent and you decide to commercialize it, very soon, you will discover that very thing you gather with God's talent without serving Him will amount to nothing.

If you cannot give, God understands, if you cannot give but have to give, God understands too. But the principles of God are unchanging and they work because they are God's words for the universe. Just like the law of gravity, which says that whatever you throw up must come down, if you learn to give, you will be blessed. That is why you have unbelievers who are rich. They are called philanthropists because they help others. Since they do that with their money, there is a law that God has put down, which they key into it and begin to prosper in it while some believers suffer.

STEPS TO FINANCIAL FREEDOM

1. You must aggressively and violently deal with the power of poverty.
2. You must never allow money to be number one in your life.
3. Avoid debt. A debtor is always a slave.
4. Seek God's leading in what you do. Do not just embark on things; pray and get a divine leading before you start.
5. High integrity and honesty must be in everything you are doing so that you can have financial freedom.

6. Give unto God as documented and enjoined in the Scriptures.

The Bible says you must give thankfully, systematically, lovingly, proportionately to what you have and selflessly when you are giving to God. Many multimillionaires and multibillionaires are in the house of God counting marbles because they are ignorant of these principles or they do not follow them. And on the last day when they get to God, God will say to them, "You were supposed to build this or that, you were supposed to help this or that or do this or that but here you are a failure because you did not know who you were."

You need to aggressively demand your financial freedom because if you are not financially free, you are not free. No matter what ideas you have, you cannot succeed without money. If you allow the devil to be stealing your money, he can paralyze your life. If you do not secure what God has given you, the enemy will take it away from you. You must understand these principles.

Before you take the prayer points below confess any sin that has to do with finances to the Lord. Perhaps you do not pay your tithe, or give any offering; you come to the Lord empty, or you give the Lord tips as if you were giving a beggar. If you will confess these sins and promise that you will be His partner and make restitution, you will be amazed at what God will do with your life. It is a tragedy when you are supposed to be a mountain mover, but the hands with which you should pull down the mountain have been cut off by poverty. Ask the Lord to forgive you. Perhaps you make pledges and vows but do not fulfill them, ask the Lord to forgive you.

FINANCIAL DELIVERANCE

Prayer Points

1. Foundational poverty, you are a liar, die, in the name of Jesus.
2. My wealth buried in the earth, come forth, in the name of Jesus.
3. Every arrow of witchcraft fired into my prosperity, die, in the name of Jesus.
4. Garment of poverty, catch fire, in the name of Jesus.
5. You financial killer of my father's house, I am not your candidate, therefore, die, in the name of Jesus.
6. Expected and unexpected financial breakthrough, locate me by fire, in the name of Jesus.
7. Poverty activator dreams, hear the word of the Lord, scatter, in the name of Jesus.

OTHER BOOKS BY DR.D.K.OLUKOYA

1. 20 Marching Order To Fulfill Your Destiny
2. 30 Things The Anointing Can Do For You
3. 30 Poverty-Destroying Keys
4. 30 Prophetic Arrows From Heaven
5. A-Z Of Complete Deliverance
6. Abraham's Children In Bondage
7. Basic Prayer Patterns
8. Battle Against the Wasters
9. Be Prepared
10. Becoming Extraordinary Among The Ordinary
11. Bewitchment Must Die
12. Biblical Principles Of Dream Interpretation
13. Biblical Principles Of Long Life
14. Born Great, But Tied Down
15. Born To Overcome
16. Breaking Bad Habits
17. Breakthrough Prayers For Business Professionals
18. Bringing Down The Power Of God
19. Brokenness
20. Can God Trust You?
21. Can God?
22. Charge Your Battery
23. Command The Morning
24. Connecting To The God Of Breakthroughs
25. Consecration Commitment & Loyalty

Other Books By Dr.D.K.Olukoya

26. Contending For The Kingdom
27. Criminals In The House Of God
28. Dancers At The Gate Of Hell
29. Dealing With The Evil Powers Of Your Father's House
30. Dealing With The Powers Of The Night
31. Dealing With Tropical Demons
32. Dealing With Local Satanic Technology
33. Dealing With Witchcraft Barbers
34. Dealing With Unprofitable Roots
35. Dealing With Hidden Curses
36. Dealing With Destiny Vultures
37. Dealing With Satanic Exchange
38. Dealing With Destiny Thieves
39. Deliverance Of The Head
40. Deliverance Of The Tongue
41. Deliverance: God's Medicine Bottle
42. Deliverance From Evil Load
43. Deliverance From Spirit Husband And Spirit Wife
44. Deliverance From The Limiting Power
45. Deliverance From Triangular Powers
46. Deliverance From Evil Foundation
47. Deliverance Of The Brain
48. Deliverance Of The Conscience
49. Deliverance By Fire
50. Destiny Clinic

Other Books By Dr.D.K.Olukoya

51. Destroying Satanic Marks
52. Disgracing Soul Hunters
53. Disgracing Water Spirits
54. Divine Yellow Card
55. Divine Prescription For Your Total Immunity
56. Divine Military Training
57. Dominion Prosperity
58. Drawers Of Powers From The Heavenlies
59. Evil Appetite
60. Evil Umbrella
61. Facing Both Ways
62. Failure In The School Of Prayer
63. Fire For Life's Journey
64. Fire For Spiritual Battles For The 21st Century Army
65. For We Wrestle...
66. Freedom Indeed
67. Fresh Fire(Bilingual Book In French)
68. God's Keys To A Happy Life
69. Handling the Sword of Deliverance
70. Healing Through Prayers
71. Holiness Unto The Lord
72. Holy Fever
73. Holy Cry
74. Hour Of Decision
75. How To Find The Presence of God
76. How To Obtain Personal Deliverance

Other Books By Dr.D.K.Olukoya

77. How To Pray When Surrounded By The Enemies
78. I Am Moving Forward
79. Idol Of The Heart
80. Igniting Your Inner Fire
81. Captured by the Slave Master
82. Is This What They Died For?
83. Killing Your Goliath By Fire
84. Killing The Serpent Of Frustration
85. Let God Answer By Fire
86. Let Fire Fall
87. Limiting God
88. Looking Unto Jesus
89. Lord, Behold Their Threatening
90. Madness Of The Heart
91. Making Your Way Through The Traffic Jam Of Life
92. Meat For Champions
93. Medicine For Winners
94. My Burden For The Church
95. Open Heaven Through Holy Disturbance
96. Overpowering Witchcraft
97. Passing Through The Valley Of The Shadow Of Death
98. Paralysing The Rider And The Horse
99. Personal Spiritual Check-Up
100. Possessing The Tongue Of Fire

Other Books By Dr.D.K.Olukoya

101. 100.Power To Recover Your Birthright
102. Power Against Captivity
103. Power Against Coffin Spirits
104. Power Against Unclean Spirits
105. Power Against The Mystery Of Wickedness
106. Power Against Destiny Quenchers
107. Power Against Dream Criminals
108. Power Against Local Wickedness
109. Power Against Marine Spirits
110. Power Against Spiritual Terrorists
111. Power To Recover Your Lost Glory
112. Power To Disgrace The Oppressor
113. Power Must Change Hands
114. Power Must Change Hands (Prayer Points From 1995-2010)
115. Power To Shut Satanic Doors
116. Power Against The Mystery Of Wickedness
117. Power Against Business Bewitchment
118. Power Of Brokenness
119. Pray Your Way To Breakthroughs
120. Prayer To Make You Fulfill Your Divine Destiny
121. Prayer Strategies For Spinsters And Bachelors
122. Prayer Warfare Against 70 Mad Spirits
123. Prayer Is The Battle
124. Prayer To Kill Enchantment

Other Books By Dr.D.K.Olukoya

125. Prayer Rain
126. Prayer To Destroy Diseases And Infirmities
127. Prayer For Open Heavens
128. Prayers To Move From Minimum To Maximum
129. Praying Against Foundational Poverty
130. Praying Against The Spirit Of The Valley
131. Praying In The Storm
132. Praying To Dismantle Witchcraft
133. Praying To Destroy Satanic Roadblocks
134. Principles Of Conclusive Prayers
135. Principles Of Prayer
136. Raiding The House Of The Strongman
137. Release From Destructive Covenants
138. Revoking Evil Decrees
139. Safeguarding Your Home
140. Satanic Diversion Of The Black Race
141. Secrets Of Spiritual Growth & Maturity
142. Self-Made Problems (Bilingual Book In French)
143. Seventy Rules Of Spiritual Warfare
144. Seventy Sermons To Preach To Your Destiny
145. Silencing The Birds Of Darkness
146. Slave Masters
147. Slaves Who Love Their Chains
148. Smite The Enemy And He Will Flee
149. Speaking Destruction Unto The Dark Rivers

Other Books By Dr.D.K.Olukoya

150. Spiritual Education
151. Spiritual Growth And Maturity
152. Spiritual Warfare And The Home
153. Stop Them Before They Stop You
154. Strategic Praying
155. Strategy Of Warfare Praying
156. Students In The School Of Fear
157. Symptoms Of Witchcraft Attack
158. Taking The Battle To The Enemy's Gate
159. The Amazing Power Of Faith
160. The God Of Daniel (Bilingual Book In French)
161. The God Of Elijah (Bilingual Book In French)
162. The Vagabond Spirit
163. The Unlimited God
164. The Wealth Transfer Agenda
165. The Way Of Divine Encounter
166. The Unconquerable Power
167. The Baptism By Fire
168. The Battle Against The Spirit Of Impossibility
169. The Chain Breaker
170. The Dining Table Of Darkness
171. The Enemy Has Done This
172. The Evil Cry Of Your Family Idol
173. The Fire Of Revival
174. The School Of Tribulation
175. The Gateway To Spiritual Power
176. The Great Deliverance

Other Books By Dr. D.K. Olukoya

177. The Internal Stumbling Block
178. The Lord Is A Man Of War
179. The Lost Secret Of The Church
180. The Militant Christian
181. The Mystery Of The Mobile Curses
182. The Mystery Of The Mobile Temple
183. The Prayer Eagle
184. The Power Of Aggressive Prayer Warriors
185. The Power Of Priority
186. The Tongue Trap
187. The Terrible Agenda
188. The Scale Of The Almighty
189. The Hidden Viper
190. The Star In Your Sky
191. The Star Hunters
192. The Spirit Of The Crab
193. The Snake In The Power House
194. The Slow Learners
195. The University Of Champions
196. The Skeleton In The Grandfather's Cupboard
197. The Serpentine Enemies
198. The Secrets Of Greatness
199. The Seasons Of Life
200. The Pursuit Of Success
201. Tied Down In The Spirit
202. Too Hot To Handle
203. Turnaround Breakthrough

Other Books By Dr.D.K.Olukoya

204. Unprofitable Foundations
205. Victory Over Your Greatest Enemies
206. Victory Over Satanic Dreams
207. Violent Prayers Against Stubborn Situations
208. War At The Edge Of Breakthroughs
209. Wasted At The Market Square Of Life
210. Wasting The Wasters
211. Wealth Must Change Hands
212. What You Must Know About The House Fellowship
213. When The Battle Is From Home
214. When Your labour needs deliverance
215. When You Need A Change
216. When The Deliverer Needs Deliverance
217. When Things Get Hard
218. When You Are Knocked Down
219. When Your Are Under Attack
220. When The Enemy Hides
221. When God Is Silent
222. Where Is Your Faith?
223. While Men Slept
224. Woman! Thou Art Loosed
225. Why Problems Come Back
226. Your Battle And Your Strategy
227. Your Foundation And Your Destiny
228. Your Mouth And Your Deliverance
229. Your Mouth And Your Warfare

Other Books By Dr.D.K.Olukoya

YORUBA PUBLICATIONS
1. Adura Agbayori
2. Adura Ti Nsi Oke Ni Dii
3. Ojo Adura

FRENCH PUBLICATIONS
1. Pluie De Prière
   Esprit De Vagabondage
2. En Finir Avec Les Forces Maléfiques De La Maison De Ton Père
3. Que L'envoutement Périsse
4. Frappez L'adversaire et il Fuira
5. Comment Recevoir La Délivrance Du Mari Et De La Femme De Nuit
6. Comment Se Délivrer Soimeme
7. Pouvoir Contre Les Terroristes Spirituels
8. Prières De Percées Pour Les Homes D'affaires
9. Prier Jusqu'a Remporter La Victoire
10. Prières Violentes Pour Humilier Les Problèmes Opiniâtres
11. Prière Pour Détruire Les Maladies Et Les Infirmités
12. Le Combat Spiritual Et Le Foyer
13. Bilan Spiritual Personnel
14. Victories Sur Les Rêves Sataniques
15. Prier De Combat Contre 70 Esprits Déchaînés
16. La Déviation Satanique De La Race Noire

Other Books By Dr.D.K.Olukoya

17. Ton Combat Et Ta Stratégie
18. Votre Fondement Et Votre Destin
19. Révoquer Les Décrets Maléfiques
20. Cantique Des Cantiques
21. Le Mauvais Cri Des Idoles
22. Quand Les Choses Deviennent Difficiles
23. Les Stratégies De Prier Pour Les Célibataires
24. Se Libérer Des Alliances Maléfiques
25. Démanteler La Sorcellerie
26. La Délivrance: Le Flacon De Médicament De Dieu
27. La Délivrance De La Tête
28. Commander Le Matin
29. Ne Grand Mais Lie
30. Pouvoir Contre Les Demons Tropicaux
31. Le Programme De Transfert Des Richesse
32. Les étudiants à l'école De La Peur
33. L'étoile Dans Votre Ciel
34. Les Saisons De La Vie
35. Femme Tu Es Libérée

ANNUAL 70 DAYS PRAYER AND FASTING PUBLICATIONS
1. Prayers That Bring Miracles

Other Books By Dr.D.K.Olukoya

2. Let God Answer By Fire
3. Prayers To Mount Up With Wings As Eagles
4. Prayers That Bring Explosive Increase
5. Prayers For Open Heavens
6. Prayers To You Fulfill Your Divine Destiny
7. Prayers That Make God To Answer And Fight By Fire
8. Prayers That Bring Unchallengeable Victory And Breakthrough Rainfall Bombardments
9. Prayers That Bring Dominion Prosperity And Uncommon Success
10. Prayers That Bring Power And Overflowing Progress
11. Prayers That Bring Laughter And Enlargement Breakthroughs
12. Prayers That Bring Uncommon Favour And Breakthroughs
13. Prayers That Bring Unprecedented Greatness & Unmatchable Increase
14. Prayers That Bring Awesome Testimonies And Turnaround Breakthroughs
15. Prayers That Brings Dominion Celebration and Supernatural Open Doors.

Made in the USA
Middletown, DE
07 September 2021